Recruitment & Staffing Revealed

Recruitment & Staffing Revealed

Discover Exactly What Is Involved With Starting & Scaling Your Niche' Recruitment and Staffing Business

By:

DEE WILLIAMS

An Imprint of Identifize Consulting | Staffingpreneurs Academy

INDIVIDUAL
AUDACITY PUBLISHING

For information, address Individual Audacity Publishing, 11175 Cicero Dr., Ste 100, Alpharetta, GA 30022-0003. Visit: http://individualaudacitypublishing.com

An imprint of Dee Williams and Identifize Consulting. This author is represented by Individual Audacity publishing, Alpharetta, GA.

Individual Audacity Publishing books may be purchased for educational, business, or sales promotional use. For information, please email the Special Markets Division at SMSales@individualaudacitypublishing.com.

FIRST EDITION

Library of Congress Cataloging-in-Publication Data has been applied for.

Paperback ISBN: 978-0-9997973-6-5
Ebook – Kindle ISBN: 978-0-9997973-5-8

Printed in the United States of America

For every entrepreneur who has a dream to do something bigger than wat they ever imagined. You have the power to change the way we live. I believe in you.

TABLE OF CONTENTS

1.	NICHE' SEGMENTATION	1
2.	STARTUP & SCALING	3
3.	STRATEGY DEVELOPMENT	4
4.	PROCESSES, POLICIES, & FRAMEWORKS	8
5.	FORMS & CONTRACTS	10
6.	FUNDING & BACK OFFICE	12
7.	TECHNOLOGY & AUTOMATION	14
8.	BRANDING	16
9.	MARKETING	18
10.	SALES & BUSINESS DEVELOPMENT	22
11.	CANDIDATE ATTRACTION	24
12.	SOURCING SEARCH	26
13.	TALENT PIPELINING	28
14.	RECRUITMENT	30
15.	PLACEMENT & STAFFING	32
16.	FOLLOW-UP	34
17.	METRICS & SCALING	36
18.	TEAM TRAINING & DEVELOPMENT	38
19.	INTERNAL HIRING	42
20.	NEXT STEPS	44

What's Involved in Starting and Scaling a Niche' Recruitment and Staffing Business?

So you're in the market to start or scale a niche' recruitment and staffing business. Congratulations because this is one of the best profitable and socially impactful businesses on the market today! You will have the awesome opportunity to impact hundreds of lives and help companies all across the globe solve world challenges. This is so exciting right? I know!

Okay, so I want to get you prepared for this journey. You're either reading this because you're interested in starting your own recruitment and staffing business, or because you already have one and you're looking for ways to turn it around, or help it grow. Either way, I'm here to help you gain some clarity on what you need to ensure your business is working.

This book is going to be super helpful for you to see where you are and what's missing so that you can see where you want and need to be in the near future. Just to get the specifics out the way, YOU CAN start this business, YOU CAN this business around, YOU CAN grow this business, right now with direction, clarity, and some massive passion to action! Whooo!!!

Now, when we work with consulting clients and even when teaching various classes, we always start from a

BIG PICTURE VIEW of the business because it's important to view your business as a whole, to understand what areas of the business are functioning at its fullest capacity and which areas of the business need help.

Today, this quick guide will give you an understanding of each area of the business. This is a great process for you to really take a great look at what you need to do to breathe life into your niche' recruitment and staffing business. I'm really excited for you to read.

Ready to get started?

Awesomeness

1

NICHE' SEGMENTATION

Knowing who you want to do business with, what they want and need, why, and how you can help among other factors is something you need and want to know before you ever start this business. And if you already have your business up and running, then you should be revisiting these questions on a daily basis.

Listen, understanding your market is what will help you to consistently increase sales, bypass operational stagnation, and decease the chances of you experiencing financial deterioration in your business. It's like that bonus pack of vitamin C that you add to your water, right? It will help give your business purpose and direction to not only live, but to scale and thrive!

NOTE: You should have strong goals around who you want to do business with.

Having a strong niche' is the foundational point of your business allowing you to create key strategies that will take your business further and faster than your competition. When you choose a niche' YOU will become the external disruption for your competitors, and that's how you create market share.

Do you hear me? Do you understand the value of you establishing a niche, and not trying to service everyone or anyone who will do business with you?

Listen, establishing a niche' is one of the major things that will set you apart from the competition – never forget that. It IS your key competitive edge!

Speaking of competition…it's also important to know who your competition is within your niche market, what they are doing, why, and how much they charge for their solutions. When you understand what your competitors are doing, you can find ways to offer a version of what there are offering, but better offering your niche'. Think about it… [i]McDonalds was created in 1940 as a restaurant and then hamburger stand and later a corporate franchise in 1955. [ii]Burger King came along in 1953 selling the same thing – BURGERS! Now, who am I to say which is better (I'll leave that up to you), but what I will say is when you come after the competition, especially if you listen to what your market wants, likes and dislikes, you can now create a similar product, but better.

Understand that once you begin to ponder these questions, you will be able to create amazingly awesome strategies for your business to implement, right now.

Question For You: What do you currently have in place for this area of your business?

2

STARTUP & SCALING

You're either starting or scaling, and in both situations, this part of the business is never 100% complete. Startup is not just about legalizing the business, it's about knowing your mission, purpose, **goals** and **objectives**. It's about creating your vision and theme, based on all of those things encompassed with your **WHY**. Don't be afraid to take your time building the foundation of your business. And if you already have your business established, when was the last time you revisited who you are, what you stand for and why you are doing what you do?

This is your foundation, just like when building your house. Would you live in a house without a solid structure? Without floors, walls and ceilings? Of course not! So why would you run your business that way?

Take the time to build your foundation from the very beginning and then take more time to ensure your foundation is always sound, strong and sturdy. You will thank me later for this.

Question For You: What do you currently have in place for this area of your business?

3

STRATEGY DEVELOPMENT

Do you remember the movie [iii]The Waterboy with actor Adam Sandler? Adam plays a character by the name of Bobby Boucher (pronounced "Boo-SHAY") who was the water boy for a local college football team. Now this team was a losing football team with a winning coach Klein, except coach Klein was no longer winning because his college rival took his secret playbook of winning strategies many years ago. Let me tell you, Coach Klein was obsessed with this little green book of playbook strategies because he understood the importance of having a number of winning strategies. It gave him the confidence he needed to crush the competition, and that's what I want you to have.

Winning strategies that YOU create for your business is what will set you apart from your competition.

It's super important that you are always developing new strategies for you to reach the social, production, and financial goals of your business as well as modifying goals that you've already created to ensure execution is guaranteed and goals are reached.

WHAT'S INVOLVED IN STARTING AND SCALING A NICHE' RECRUITMENT AND STAFFING BUSINESS

As a whole, there should be a major BIG PICTURE review once a quarter, at the very least. I'm sure you're thinking, "haven't we already covered strategy?" Well, yes and no. Based on my experience teaching professionals how to start and scale their very own niche' recruitment and staffing business,

I've learned that the "real" strategy planning takes place here, because your strategy is always based on #1 Niche' Segmentation and #2 your Mission, Goals and Objectives. So, what I want you to do at this point is to take all of the information that you've gathered and see how it fits into what your market wants and needs. I want you to start calling people and asking questions to find out how you can revise and create. What issues are your clients and candidates experiencing in the market as a whole and from your competitors? How can you fix it? Can you offer training, a mobile app, a special checklist or spreadsheet? Can you develop a service specifically to cater to the needs of your market? What's missing? Write is down and draw it out.

Remember: there is not one winning championship team on this planet that does not have a playbook of strategies (notice the "s" on the end of the word). That means, don't settle for just one strategy. Write as many as you can think of down and keep adding to your playbook as long as you're in business. You don't have to implement them all at once, but at least you will have focus and less risk of experiencing operational stagnation.

Go as far as looking at what other industries are doing and take their strategies and put them to use in your business model if it makes sense. If it has already been done and it works, Test it! Now go out and be strategic with some majorly winning plays!

Question For You: What do you currently have in place for this area of your business?

4

PROCESSES, POLICIES, & FRAMEWORKS

When I help newbies get started with this business, they typically don't think about creating and implementing polices or frameworks. While most are obsessed with learning the processes, many don't want to take the time to document them, and they hire us to help them, however, having these tools is one thing, enforcing them on a regular basis is another.

NOTE: Having processes, policies and frameworks to help define your business will ensure healthy and sustainable growth.

So, if you're just getting started, I want to help prevent you from experiencing the bottlenecks that already established agencies experience, when they don't have and enforce, strong polices, processes and frameworks within their business. See, you're lucky you're getting the heads up.

Because, it's not just operational. It goes deeper than that. It's also cultural. One of the main reasons you want to ensure you're thinking about and documenting and enforcing strong polices, processes and frameworks is to help build and define the culture of

9

your company. I'm not sure what your goals are for your business, but your potential is endless. And if you're looking to be one of the 1,631 recruitment and staffing businesses who are generating more than $10M in revenue within the U.S., then you want to start early, setting the business up for scalability and growth.

Don't be one of those business owners who only focus on making the money. That's not a great strategy to have because when the market changes or technology shifts or legal regulations began to take their toll, you will need to have a structure in place (along with a great leadership team) to keep you afloat and sail with confidence.

Take it seriously. Start creating them now. It will be one of the best things that you do for your business.

Question For You: What do you currently have in place for this area of your business?

5

FORMS & CONTRACTS

Compliance is key to running a successful niche' recruitment and staffing business. When you're compliant, you're winning not just today, but in the future too. You see, it's easy to bypass compliance now, but in the future when it hits you in the butt, you will think back and wonder where you failed. I will tell you now, don't play around with compliance. Cover Your Ass and stay compliant.

Make sure you don't do business with ANYONE unless you have a written contract, and while you don't truly have a written contract between you and your candidates, presenting them with a Right-to-Represent is a great way to let your candidates know you're serious about doing business, and you're serious about doing business with them.

When you have contracts in place, you're ultimately solidifying your candidate and client relationships on paper. Oh, one more thing before I move on. Please make sure you read your contracts thoroughly. I see a lot of students purchase contracts or have their attorney write and review the contracts, but the Staffingpreneur never once takes the time to read it. Until the hiring manager or the legal counsel of the client company mentions an error that they see. You become more powerful when you know and understand what you're presenting.

Question For You: What do you currently have in place for this area of your business?

6

FUNDING & BACK OFFICE

Years ago, if you wanted to start a staffing business where you would hire people to work for companies, you needed tons of startup cash to bring your business to market. However today, things are a bit easier and more convenient.

Let me give you a bit of advice here. If you're just starting out in this business it's important for you, (especially in the early stages) to focus on the activities that will generate revenue in your business. That's why I recommend that you partner with a great Employee Payroll Funding company who also provides back office support solutions.

Partnering with an employee payroll company will allow you the flexibility you need to hire and expand now and in the future. It's also a great strategic play for you to add to your playbook of strategies. It's called leverage, and it will give you the leverage that you need to focus on what's important RIGHT NOW and that's building the business.

Recruitment is just one side of the business right. There is a very low overhead when you're only working the recruiting side of the business, but a prime play like working with an Employee Payroll Funding Company will help you to remove all your fears and headaches around the cost of offering and setting up the staffing side of the business, where you employ temporary and contract employees on behalf of your customers.

It will give you the flexibility to add this powerful solution to your business model without having to stress about onboarding employees and running payroll, especially when you're only a one or two man/woman business. Today, you have the power to have a support system that will work with you to ensure you can focus on the important stuff like getting clients, finding and placing amazing talent.

Once you've established your core strategies, have some strong processes in place, and have some wins under your belt, then you can think about taking on the payroll and back office responsibilities, but in the beginning, just focus on building the business.

Question For You: What do you currently have in place for this area of your business?

7

TECHNOLOGY & AUTOMATION

I was recently working with a company based in Dubai who had a focus on placing IT talent – cyber security talent to be exact. And one of the first questions I asked was, what technology are you using? What ATS are you using? What email marketing platform are you using? The silence over the phone answered my questions immediately, but I patiently waited for an answer. After about 30-seconds or so, I heard a faint response in the distance saying, "nothing Dee – Microsoft Excel". Microsoft Excel? Can you believe it? While Excel will always be a great tool to manage the business, it's not robust enough to give you the competitive advantage you need, to really make this business work. It's 2018 and technology rules the world (especially data-based technology). It's time to think bigger.

Listen, do you understand that one of the reasons [iv]Km art loss to Walmart and Target is because of their lack of vision around implementing and staying on top of technology (amongst, a number of other things as well), but you get the point? Do you want to end up like Kmart? Of course not! You want to be here for the long haul. You want this business to be around long enough for your children to run the business, like a niche mother-daughter client of mine in Oklahoma City, OK. This IS a legacy business, so stay competitive.

Now, there are so many ways to automate your niche' recruitment and staffing business today that work directly with the processes and tasks you've created for your business.

If you're still working old-school with the Excel spreadsheets, then it's time to upgrade.

These technologies will help you stay organized, stay compliant and stay competitive. And believe me, you WANT to be competitive and move at the rate that your competitors, clients and candidates are moving, or faster even! This quickest way to fall-short, loose revenue and simply grow stale is by not implementing technology that will help automate your business - in just about every area.

Question For You: What do you currently have in place for this area of your business?

8

BRANDING

Do me a favor. Think about the last time you saw or heard about a product or service that you had an interest in. What's the first thing you did when you went to research it. You went online right? You went looking for the website, reviews and maybe even the company's social media profiles. And once you got there and got the information you needed, you made an informed decision as to whether or not the company was worthy and viable enough to have your money. And if you gave them your money, it's because they positioned themselves to you based on their brand image. And trust me, your brand image is EVERYTHING in today's society.

Listen, the brand that you create for your business is all about how you wish to represent yourself and your business to the world. Your brand footprint is how people will find you online and offline. Your brand is also what sets you apart from your competition. It helps tell your story of how you got to where you are today and where you plan to go.

Today, with local stores closing, cybersecurity being on the rise, and content dominating the internet, it's super important that you present yourself to the world with a strong professional brand image.

One that says, "I can solve your hiring issues, I am trustworthy, and I can deliver with ease. You will be happy parting with me! Here, let me show you we know what we are talking about. Let me help you!"

Now, while this is a separate function than marketing, the two strategically work very closely hand-in-hand so take your brand seriously. Don't obsess over it, but make sure it speaks to who you are, what you do, and where you plan to take your customers.

Question For You: What do you currently have in place for this area of your business?

9

MARKETING

A company out of Houston, TX reached out to me with a major problem. They said, "Dee! We've been in business for 3 months and have not received one phone call. The business is broken. What should we do?" So, I asked, "Can you tell me about your marketing strategy? Where are you advertising and what are you doing to go out and get what you want?" Boy, you would have thought I asked them for their blood-type and first-born child. They looked at me with the most confused look on their face. But it wasn't their facial expression that got me, it was their deep silence around the topic that really took me back. So, I asked again, and this time the Staffingpreneur owner said to me, "you mean we need to have a marketing strategy?"

Listen, you can have the best brand and the best business model, products, services and candidates even, but if nobody knows about them, then how will your business succeed? Guess what? It probably won't – at least not in today's economy. You must create strategies to get the word out about your business online **and** offline. This is how you will be able to attract new clients, and the very best talent in your niche industry.

When you are strategically and deliberately marketing your business, you're letting the industry know that you're here and you're here to bring value.

Word of Caution: Marketing today is not about spamming people with your sales messages. Nope, that's the way it used to be done, but thank goodness, we're evolving as a people, and because there is so much information out there, being strategic in your marketing message ALWAYS consists of providing your market audience with value.

My marketing mentor ᵛGary Vaynerchuk created a method called Jab, Jab, Jab, Right Hook which represents the amount of value that you should be delivering in your marketing messages before you should ever ask for or market the sale. That's right, it's no longer just about the sale - it's now about giving value to build the relationship. It's about informing your client market to help them make the proper choice on the type of talent they should hire and when. It's about informing your candidate market about the types of jobs that are out there, what companies are looking for, as well as when and how to search for their next career opportunity. It's about showing people you are the "go-to" resource for finding and hiring a specific type of talent. Use articles, checklists, videos, eBooks, comparisons, diagrams and more to help educate your clients and build trust.

And guess what? I recently read that, "[vi] 75% of the executives said they watch work-related videos on business-related websites at least weekly and more than half, 52% watch work-related videos on YouTube." so as you can see, video is the most critical source for delivering information to executives today, from your business website.

Remember, marketing works very closely with branding as well as Sales & Business Development, so close that you cannot have one without the other. Claim your position, within your market today, with confidence and get to marketing!!

Question For You: Now, how does your current process foster building value-based relationships? What do you currently have in place for this area of your business?

WHAT'S INVOLVED IN STARTING AND SCALING A NICHE' RECRUITMENT AND STAFFING BUSINESS

10

SALES & BUSINESS DEVELOPMENT

If branding lets the world know who you are, and marketing draws people to you, then sales and business development is the process of you going out and getting the business. That's right! While your marketing machine is running in the background, it's also your job to go out and find the companies, employers and hiring managers who need your help (whether they know they need your help or not).

Many newbies feel this is the most intimidating part of the business process, but the reality is, if you're thinking that way, then you're not thinking like a CEO. And YOU are the CEO of YOUR business.

Listen, your sales process will help you drive growth, and depending on your mindset, your company will either be delivered and viewed as an order-taker firm or a firm that is a subject matter expert (SME) in your particular niche field, helping customers gain insight on what's going on in the market and what they can do to combat market challenges. When you have a strong sales process in place that focuses on solving key issues like retention, quality, and growth, you will see that the job orders will flow like the Hudson River and sales will not be so intimidating anymore.

Remember: A strong sales process is important, but the ability to build the relationship while consistently showing value is <u>imperative</u>, which is why today you will find that your sales and marketing strategies go hand-in-hand. Your marketing strategy will deliver content to inform your potential clients, giving them something to think of while introducing them to you (which is why your branding is important) and then sales comes along to reiterate what you've already shared via your marketing strategies and to inform your potential clients of their options.

Again, please don't waste your time simply creating sales videos. They rarely work in today's market. Create informational videos that offer content that answers your client's questions and addresses their talent shortage issues. Help your clients see you as the "go-to" resources for their niche' recruitment and staffing challenges.

Question For You: What do you currently have in place for this area of your business?

11

CANDIDATE ATTRACTION

Just like marketing and sales work together, so does candidate attraction and sourcing. Candidate attraction is all about how you attract the very best talent on the market to your niche' recruitment and staffing business, and to your client's open positions.

When working in the Professional Solutions space, companies are no longer in the market to find and pay for mediocre talent – heck, the temp side either. Look, if you're thinking this business today is as easy as posting a job online and submitting the resume to the client, you are sadly mistaken. Especially since most companies are already posting their jobs on job boards such as Indeed.com, Monster.com, etc. They don't need you to do for them, what they can already do for themselves. What they need is a resource that can help them sift through the mediocre talent and find them the absolute best talent on the market. It's your network and networking that will help you identify the best talent. It's your technical skills, your ability to research and tap into various tribes, that will set you apart.

It's the places that you post to, that the client companies don't know about. It's the relationships that you build with talent that will set you apart.

My question to you is, "do you need to update your candidate strategy?" Because candidate attraction is all about attracting talent that cannot be found or recruited by your clients. That is one of your major market value solutions that will allow you to separate yourself from the competition.

Take it seriously and go and attract some amazing talent.

Question For You: What do you currently have in place for this area of your business?

12

SOURCING SEARCH

When you understand your market, you now know where to find the best talent. Like I stated earlier, job boards are played out (for the most part) for recruitment and staffing agencies (unless you know how to use them strategically, or maybe if you're filling a ton of temp or contract orders). Your sourcing work is all about finding and securing the "hidden A Player" talent, especially if you're playing in the professional solutions space.

Have you ever noticed that on splits boards all of the hardest positions are listed there? Why? Because companies cannot find the talent they are looking for to fill the positions, so they are reaching out for help to make that happen. Now, if you have the same talent that they already have (from the job boards), you bring no real value. That's why it's important to understand the difference between candidate attraction and talent sourcing, which is all about going out and getting the talent that companies actually want to hire. Being bold and deliberate about who you want to build relationships with to place now or in the future – that's a smart choice.

Companies don't want to waste their time, money and resources on hiring mediocre talent! They want "A Players" (at least most of them do), so networking, using the data you've accumulated and collecting data to help you find pockets of rare talent will make you invaluable, especially if you're focusing on a single position or two.

If you want to stay in business, in today's market, being able to find and build solid relationships with "A talent" is imperative.

Question For You: What do you currently have in place for this area of your business?

13

TALENT PIPELINING

I have a client in New York who I absolutely love because he's young and not afraid to do or try anything in his niche' recruitment and staffing business. His focus is on healthcare placing registered nurses and physical therapists. Well, when he first got started, he said to me, "Dee, I need contracts. Candidates are nice, but I will find them easily, what I need are clients and job orders." How eager we are when we are young and still maturing. I responded lightly, because I knew whatever I said would not matter much.

This young man needed to experience the business first! So, I waited and watched. And sure-enough less than 30-days passed and he had an opportunity to fill a number of positions with a single client. He was armed with job orders, excited, and ready to do business! Whoooo!

Now let's time-skip two-to-three weeks ahead, where I followed up with him to see how things were going. You know my biggest question was, "how's it going along with your new positions? How many submittals have you made? How many interviews with the clients? Have you made any placements?" He responded as if he was confessing his sins and said,

"The Company filled the positions on their own. I didn't present candidates fast enough." He said, *"You were right! I need to focus on building my candidate pipeline more. I want to be able to have a network of candidates' that I know or can at least call, I don't really know anyone yet. I wasn't prepared to fill the positions because I really didn't know anyone."*

That was a HUGE learning lesson for my client, and one I want you to learn without having to disappoint the client or embarrass yourself first.

Remember, your services are typically needed because of your network, the talent that you and your team know and have built relationships with, and your ability to secure that talent throughout the hiring process and beyond. It's your job to have more than one candidate in the mix at any given time (or at least you should know where to go to access your pool of talent, especially "A Talent"). Remember: It's your network and the resources that you use to find and secure specialized talent is what will ultimately set you apart.

Question For You: What do you currently have in place for this area of your business?

14

RECRUITMENT

This is one of the core services that you offer as a Staffingpreneur. The ability to build and sell a candidate on a relationship, as well as a temp, contract or direct hire opportunity. Trust me, this will allow you to **dominate** your market.

When you're working on the commercial side of staffing (temporary placement) almost all candidates want to speak to you when you call and when you email. However, the professional solutions market is a bit different.

When you're dealing with skilled professionals who have recruiters coming at them 10, 20, 30 times a day, they may not be as excited to hear from you. It's true that not every person you speak to will be on the market for a new career opportunity.

Even if they hate or are unhappy with their current working situation, they still may not be looking or open to moving into another position. In fact, you may meet a number of candidates who are not working, and even then, you still cannot recruit them into a position or sell them on starting a professional relationship with you?

Why? Because people are in different places within their lives. Some people (even though unhappy in their current working situation), are afraid of change. Change means new tasks, new people, new commute, new everything and the idea of starting over into a position that they know nothing about can be rather intimidating. That's why it's your job to "sell" the candidate on building that relationship with you and allowing you to be their eyes and ears on the market, for them. It's your job to understand their current situation (whether good or bad) and help lead them to the working promise land.

Also, ensuring your candidate is aware of the hiring process and where they are in the hiring process every step of the way will be a key differentiator in a world where most recruiters don't ever take the time to follow-up. And finally, understanding the importance of timing. Knowing candidates' career cycles will also help you make more quality matches now in the future.

Question For You: What do you currently have in place for this area of your business?

15

PLACEMENT & STAFFING

Recruiting talent is one thing, but getting your candidates starting is another. It's 100% your job to make sure your candidates have an easy resignation from their current position as well as a great hiring and onboarding experience into their new career opportunity. Did I mention that it's a great way to ensure the success of your niche' recruitment and staffing business?

Making sure the candidate actually shows up for the job is YOUR JOB TOO! You would be surprised at how many candidates will go through the entire hiring process, including the interviews and signing the offer letter, and never show up on the first day of work. It's great that you've filled the position, but it's not actually filled until your candidate shows up for work and stays an employee. So, don't get too comfortable at this point. You cannot predict the behavior of people nor can you control them, but you can control the recruitment process.

When you create a strong recruitment process, you are ultimately helping your clients execute a successful hire match, which by the way, will keep you in business for many years to come.

Question For You: What do you currently have in place for this area of your business?

16

FOLLOW-UP

This is the most forgotten part of the entire process, and it's a shame because there is truly fortune in the follow-up. When you stay in contact with your current clients, past clients, current clients, and your candidates before, during and after the hire, you will see your business soar far beyond anything you've ever experienced.

Think of the follow-up as key operative intelligence. Intelligence on what's going on now and what will potentially take place in the future. Not only is follow-up intelligence, it's your key to building and sustaining life-long client and candidate relationships.

Honestly, this is one of the most important parts of your business process, so start thinking about great strategy plays that will help you stay in contact with your client's and candidates for years to come. And if you're already in business, and you don't have a follow-up process, well, it's time to start thinking of one now.

Question For You: What do you currently have in place for this area of your business?

WHAT'S INVOLVED IN STARTING AND SCALING A NICHE' RECRUITMENT AND STAFFING BUSINESS

17

METRICS & SCALING

Being able to understand what it takes, how much activity it takes, to create a win in your business is extremely important to the growth of your niche' recruitment and staffing business. The proper performance metrics will give you perspective around what's working in your business and what's not working.

Knowing where you are spending your money and what members on your team are and are not producing is typically done through metrics analysis. Each and every one of your metrics should be tied to your company goals and broken down in many different phases.

Metrics are also strategic plays designed to help you lead and manage your team efficiently, provide direction and accountability, manage and increase sales, scale the business and so much more.

Each recruitment and staffing business will require and focus on different metrics depending on their business model and the strategies they've created for their business, but there are always industry standards that you can use to benchmark from.

Bottom-line, if you're looking to conduct yourself as a six, seven or even an eight-figure business, you ___will___ want to create, implement and execute strong metrics within your business.

Question For You: What do you currently have in place for this area of your business?

18

TEAM TRAINING & DEVELOPMENT

If you're going to grow and scale your business, you're eventually going to have to hire. When first starting out in this business, you will work as an Independent Business Owner in a sense where you will be doing all of the work (for most of you reading this at least). When you're in control of all production, you control the level of income you bring in the door, however, it will always be capped based on the amount of work and activity that you can produce.

Once your business graduates and is ready to go to the next level, you will run your business as an Operator, someone who needs to have a team in place, to help the business grow. You can now delegate some of the production work, increasing your output, therefore increasing your profits. When you get to this point, you will want to hire a team, and having a well-trained team will be super beneficial to your business model.

Now, before you hire your team, it's super important for you to think about how you will onboard them with the knowledge they need to be able to succeed and win! Just like you're looking for the best talent to hire for your clients, you want to be able to find the best problem-solving talent that will work for you and your business at the highest level of proficiency and care.

Some recruitment and staffing agencies hire teams who are working in other countries, some hire grads right out of college, and some hire subject matter experts. Whichever model you choose to use, ensuring your team understands the value of your business, understands the goals of your business, understands your niche' market, what services and solutions you offer and how you support your clients and candidates… is 100% imperative. So, create a training program that they will be able to access from day one! Hire a coach to help them understand how to work in the business and as well as all the things they need to remember, to be successful in their new position.

I recently came back from Brooklyn, NY where I was working with another healthcare staffing client of mine. They focus on finding exceptional talent within the mental health space placing social workers and case workers and such. Their recruiting director was leaving the company and I flew out to ensure everything he knew was documented and recorded. We then took that information back to Atlanta and created three step-by-step manuals for the business as well as a training portal to access both video and written training materials for new and current team members to access. Now, this is a company who understands the power of training, right.

Remember: The more your team knows the easier it will be for your team to deliver high-quality service solutions. Never hire without having a solid training program in place, first.

Question For You: What do you currently have in place for this area of your business?

WHAT'S INVOLVED IN STARTING AND SCALING A NICHE' RECRUITMENT AND STAFFING BUSINESS

19

INTERNAL HIRING

Hiring superstars for your clients is one thing. And hiring for yourself is another. Being able to constantly identify amazing talent that will move your business forward is a major key to your success.

Hire your team without biases. Don't look at who they have worked for in the past specifically because that means absolutely nothing. It's not who or who they have not worked for in the past that it important, but it's the performance of the work that they completed, that's of your greatest importance.

What type of skills do they have? Are they able to do the work? Can they be taught to do the work effectively? Do they have the winning personality that's needed to work in your business? Are they able to research effectively? Can they solve problems? These are the questions that you want to ask yourself as you're thinking of putting your team in place.

One more thing…don't hire until you're absolutely ready. Many Staffingpreneurs hire too fast, or wait too late to hire (trust me, I've been in both positions, and they both hurt – ouch). Knowing when it's time for you to scale and expand is imperative for the growth of your business.

Question For You: What do you currently have in place for this area of your business?

20

NEXT STEPS

As you can see, most of these areas work together to create one huge recruitment and staffing automation system. A system that can help you impact lives for many years to come as well as feed your pockets (and your children's pockets) for generations to come.

My advice to you is to be a doer (and not a dabbler). Show the world just how awesome you are and how much you dare to impact society with your niche' recruitment and staffing business.

If you feel confident with executing each area above, we're super glad you're on track to success! Do us a favor and connect with us on Facebook and share your success story. We love success stories!

However, if you want to stop struggling with the idea of where, what, how, and when. If you're afraid to start or to move your business forward, or maybe even afraid of failing. If you desire to succeed, tired of the rat race, and really want to make a difference - bottom-line, if you're ready to get the help with one or more of the above areas because you need to bring your business idea to life or take your current business to another level – we're always here to assist you.

Endnotes

[i] 'McDonalds' Wikipedia: The Free Encyclopedia, 20 April 2018, https://en.wikipedia.org/wiki/McDonald%27s

[ii] 'History of Burger King", Wikipedia, the free encyclopedia, 3 April 2018, https://en.wikipedia.org/wiki/History_of_Burger_King

[iii] 'The Water Boy' IMDb, https://www.imdb.com/title/tt0120484/

[iv] Kmart's sales have fallen off a gigantic cliff', June 9, 2015: 7:11 AM ET, https://money.cnn.com/2015/06/08/investing/kmart-sales-decline-sears-eddie-lampert/index.html

[v] Jab, Jab, Jab, Right Hook: How To Tell Your Story in a Noisy Social World, November 26, 2013, https://www.amazon.com/Jab-Right-Hook-Story-Social/dp/006227306X

[vi] 'Does Video marketing Influence Top Executives" January 11, 2017, https://www.clearcutvideos.com/does-video-marketing-influence-top-executives/

Visit Us Today:

Be an expert on your chosen Niche via online courses:
https://staffingpreneursacademy.com

Receive online and in-person consulting:
https://identifizeconsulting.com

Speak with one of our Business Creation Specialists
☎ 866-432-8801

Made in the USA
Coppell, TX
24 September 2022

83557469R00036